D0425175

The Magic School Bus Rides Again

Deep-Sea Dive

Adapted by
Samantha Brooke

Scholastic Inc.

Arnold

Dorothy Ann (D.A.)

Wanda

Carlos

Keesha

Ralphie

Jyoti

Tim

ISBN 978-1-338-25382-5

10 9 8 7 6 5 4 3 2   18 19 20 21 22
Printed in the U.S.A.   40

First printing 2018
Book design by Jessica Meltzer

Meet Ms. Frizzle!
No other teacher is like her. She takes her
class on wild science field trips.

They go on her Magic School Bus. It
twirls and whirls and can go *anywhere*.

Where will the bus take them today?

Today Ms. Frizzle's
class is visiting the ocean.

"D.A., what are you trying to catch?"
Carlos asks.

"I'm not fishing," says D.A. "I'm using
Jyoti's Smart Locket to collect **data**. It can
record temperature, **depth**, and more!"

"I can't believe Jyoti let you borrow it.
It's her favorite **gadget**," says Carlos.
"That's why I tied it to my
fishing line. See?" says
D.A. She reels in the
line. But the locket
is gone!
"Uh-oh!" she gasps.

Meanwhile, Ms. Frizzle and the rest of the class are down on the sand.

"On today's trip, we'll discover the **denizens** and **zones** of the ocean," says Tim.

"We'll find out what animals live in the ocean and which parts they live in," says Jyoti.

Suddenly, D.A. rushes over. "Jyoti! I'm sorry, I lost your locket," she cries.

"My locket is too smart to get lost. We can use a tracking device to find it!" says Jyoti.

"What about our field trip?" asks Arnold.

"We'll learn as we go. To the bus!" says Ms. Frizzle.

POOF! The bus transforms into a submarine and dives into the ocean.

"Who's ready for a dip in the intertidal zone?" asks Ms. Frizzle.

The kids put on wet suits and jump in.

"There's more life down here than just fish," Ralphie says. He sees a hermit crab, coral, and sea grass.

As D.A. looks for the locket, the **tide** pulls her deeper into the ocean.

Jyoti catches D.A.'s arm. "The tide goes in and out here. That's how this zone got its name."

"We have to follow the tide to find the locket," says D.A. "Let's go deeper."

"This is the epipelagic zone, also known as the sunlight zone," says Ms. Frizzle.

"I bet most fish live in this zone," says Wanda.

"Correct! Ninety percent of sea life is found in this zone," Ms. Frizzle explains.

"I have the locket's signal!" cries D.A. "It's down there."

But Ms. Frizzle won't let the kids go any deeper. Back on the bus, she explains. "Water is really heavy. The deeper you go, the heavier it gets. If you swam down there, the pressure would feel like a baby elephant is sitting on you."

"We can't stop now. Look! The locket is sending video," says Jyoti.

"Whoa! It's so dark down there," says Carlos.

"Water blocks sunlight. The deeper you go, the less light there is," explains Tim.

"On the bright side, the dark is full of surprises!" says Ms. Frizzle.

"I don't do surprises," cries Arnold. "Like that—!"

Suddenly, a sea monster appears in the locket's video.

"We can't get my locket if it's **guarded** by a monster!" cries Jyoti.

"That's no monster, it's a goblin shark," says Ms. Frizzle.

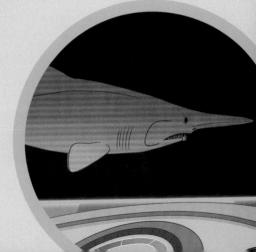

"We can't give up," says D.A. "We need more data." She searches on her tablet. "Only about five percent of the ocean has been explored! There's no data to help us."

"I'll never see my locket again," cries Jyoti.

"We can do it!" says D.A. "We need to sneak past that shark."

"We are now entering the mesopelagic zone, also called the twilight zone," Ms. Frizzle announces.

"This is my worst nightmare," Arnold cries.

"I think it's pretty. Look at all those twinkling lights," says Wanda.

"Whoa! Those lights are fish. They can make their own light?" asks Carlos.

Ms. Frizzle nods. "It's called **bioluminescence**."

"But isn't that dangerous?" asks Keesha.

Just then, the fish disappear.

"Wow! The light from above helps them **camouflage**," says Carlos.

As the class goes deeper, the bus's lights land on some red creatures.

"How come we didn't see them before? They're bright red," says Jyoti.

"When there's so little light, red is the first color to disappear," says Tim.

Ms. Frizzle turns the bus red, and it sneaks past the shark.

The bus is about to get the locket . . .
when a squid reaches out and grabs it first!

"Follow that squid!" cries D.A.

The bus dives again, chasing the squid
deeper into the ocean.

"Good news! The squid dropped the
locket," says Ms. Frizzle.

"Bad news, it fell into the bathypelagic zone," says D.A.

"We're five thousand feet down and the pressure weighs as much as an adult elephant," says Jyoti.

"And there's zero light!" says Wanda.

"That's why this is called the midnight zone," says Ms. Frizzle.

"I bet nothing lives down here," says Carlos.

"Then nothing can stop us from getting that locket!" says D.A.

"I see a light ahead. It must be the locket," says Keesha.

But there are lots of lights. Which one is the locket?

"We need to go **investigate**," says D.A.

POOF! The bus makes minisubs, and the kids head out into the deep water.

"Whoa! The lights are coming from those creepy fish!" says Tim.

The kids get closer, but the fish don't move.

"Why aren't they chasing us?" asks Arnold.

"It's like they don't have the energy to move," says Jyoti.

"It takes a lot of energy to survive down here. Instead of chasing their prey, they **lure** it with lights," says Ms. Frizzle.

"And if anything gets too close, they catch it in their big mouths," says Carlos.

Finally, the kids see the locket! But how can they grab it from inside their subs?

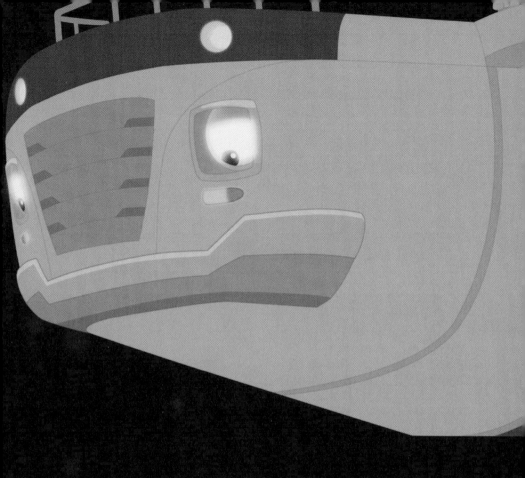

The class gets **inspiration** from the creepy fish!

"Bus, we need a big mouth!" says D.A.

The bus opens its mouth and scoops up the locket . . . and the kids in their minisubs.

"Hooray!" the kids shout.

Everyone is ready to go home, but D.A. has an idea.

"I think we should go deeper. There's a whole watery world waiting to be explored. Wanda, Ralphie, imagine all the animals you could meet," says D.A.

"Keesha and Carlos, you never back down from a challenge. Tim and Jyoti, think about the inspiration you'd find down there. And Arnold . . ." says D.A.

"No way. I want peace and quiet," he says.

"What could be quieter than the deep sea?" pleads D.A.

"Okay! Let's do it!" her friends shout.

As the bus dives deeper, it creaks under the pressure.

Suddenly Arnold shouts, "We've sprung a leak!"

"Bus, do your stuff! Fix those leaks!" says Ralphie.

"The bus can't repair itself. It used too much power to get here," says Ms. Frizzle.

Without any power, the bus sinks
deeper into the ocean.

"Welcome to the abyssalpelagic zone,"
Ms. Frizzle says.

"That means we're thirteen
thousand feet down, and
the pressure is as
heavy as twenty-five
elephants!" says D.A.

"Now we're in the hadalpelagic zone. We're thirty-six thousand feet down and the pressure is as heavy as five thousand elephants," says Ms. Frizzle.

"How can we survive?" cries Jyoti.

"If life can survive down here, so can we," says Ms. Frizzle.

"But I don't see any life," says Ralphie.

Ms. Frizzle points out some tube worms. "To survive, the tube worms change the chemicals coming from inside the earth into food," she says.

"If the worms can turn the chemicals into food, so can the bus!" says D.A.

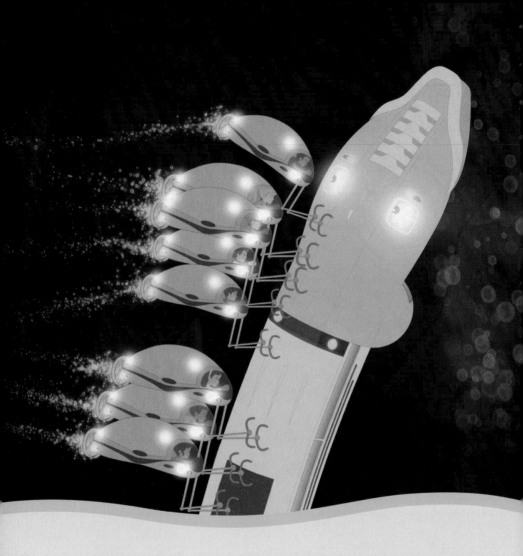

POOF! The bus transforms into a tube
worm and makes minisubs for the kids.
The kids use their minisubs to push the
bus toward the chemicals. Then the bus
turns the chemicals into energy.

"The bus is all powered up and ready to
do its stuff!" says Ms. Frizzle.

The bus turns into a jellyfish and begins to zoom up toward the surface.

"The abyssalpelagic zone . . . the bathypelagic zone . . . the mesopelagic zone . . . and finally, the epipelagic zone, otherwise known as . . . the sunlight zone!" D.A. declares as the bus breaks through the surface.

"We did it!" the class cheers.

Professor Frizzle's Glossary

Hi, I'm Ms. Frizzle's sister, Professor Frizzle. I used to teach at Walkerville Elementary. Now I do scientific research with my sidekick, Goldie. I'm always on an adventure learning new things, so here are some words for you to learn, too! Wahooo!

bioluminescence: light given off naturally by certain kinds of animals or bacteria

camouflage: a way of hiding something by covering or coloring it so that it looks like its surroundings

data: facts, figures, or other pieces of information

denizen: an animal, plant, or person living in or frequenting a particular place or area

depth: the measurement from the top of something

gadget: a small tool or device with a clever design

guard: to protect from danger or harm

inspiration: to stimulate or influence someone to do something creative

investigate: to look into carefully so as to learn the facts

lure: to attract or tempt by promising some reward

tide: the flowing of water away from or back to the land

zone: an area that is divided from other areas because of a special quality